A Note to Parents and Teachers

Dorling Kindersley Readers is a compelling programme
for be   n conjunction with
                                          perts.

Superl   mbine with engaging,
easy-to-r   approach to each subject
in the series. Each *Dorling Kindersley Reader*
is guaranteed to capture a child's interest while
developing his or her reading skills, general knowledge,
and love of reading.

The four levels of *Dorling Kindersley Readers* are
aimed at different reading abilities, enabling you to
choose the books that are exactly right for your child:

Level 1 – Beginning to read
Level 2 – Beginning to read alone
Level 3 – Reading alone
Level 4 – Proficient readers

The "normal" age at which a child begins to read
can be anywhere from three to eight years old,
so these levels are only a general guideline.

No matter which level you select, you can be sure
that you are helping your child learn to read,
then read to learn!

Dorling **DK** Kindersley

LONDON, NEW YORK, DELHI, PARIS,
MUNICH, and JOHANNESBURG

Project Editor David John
Designer Guy Harvey
Publishing Manager Cynthia O'Neill
Art Director Cathy Tincknell
Senior DTP Designer
Andrew O'Brien
Production Nicola Torode

First published in Great Britain in 2001 by
Dorling Kindersley Limited,
9 Henrietta Street,
Covent Garden, London WC23 8PS

Colour reproduction by Colourscan.
Printed and bound in China.

A CIP catalogue record for this book is
available from the British Library.

ISBN 0-7513-2985-1

All photographic images provided by
World Championship Wrestling, Inc.

see our complete catalogue at
www.dk.com

Contents

DORLING KINDERSLEY *READERS* WCW

FIT FOR THE
TITLE

Written by Michael Teitelbaum

PROFICIENT **4** READERS

A Dorling Kindersley Book

To make a champion

It's a night of WCW wrestling, and the crowds are cheering for their favourite champions. Maybe they're roaring for a heavyweight, like Scott Steiner, a cruiserweight, like Kidman, or a tag team, like Kronik.

Whichever champion the crowds support, one thing is certain – that wrestler has put in years of hard work to get where he is today.

Good habits
He may be a bad boy wrestler, but Scott Steiner has one good habit – training! It has made him fit to win the WCW heavyweight title.

Kronik
These tag team champions form a world-class partnership.

What the fans see each week is the result of sweat and sacrifice. It takes the highest level of physical conditioning to succeed. And even a wrestler who has the body and knows the right moves won't win, unless he has the right attitude, too.

WCW champions are "made", not born. The road to a WCW title takes commitment, perseverance, and a great deal of training. For most wrestlers, that road begins at a place called the Power Plant.

Kidman is a former WCW cruiserweight champion.

Nitro and **Thunder**
These shows appear on TV in the US. Viewers can enjoy top WCW action at least twice a week.

Back to school

The Power Plant is
a school, based in
Georgia, USA. Students
here don't study maths
or English. Instead, they
take classes in weight
lifting, conditioning, and aerobic
exercise – because the Power Plant
is a school for aspiring wrestlers.

The students here learn how to
wrestle safely. They study basic
wrestling skills, like how to lift,
throw, or pin an opponent.
They find out how to escape
from wrestling's toughest holds.
Most importantly, they learn the
strict mental discipline needed to
become a champion.

The Power Plant separates
serious wrestling contenders from
half-hearted pretenders.

*An instructor at the Power Plant puts some
new recruits through their paces.*

**"Give me ten
more!"**
Young wrestlers
exercise to build
strength in their
hearts, lungs,
and muscles.
They also work
out on aerobic
machines to
push themselves
to the limit.

Star pupil
Chuck
Palumbo is a
former Power
Plant student.

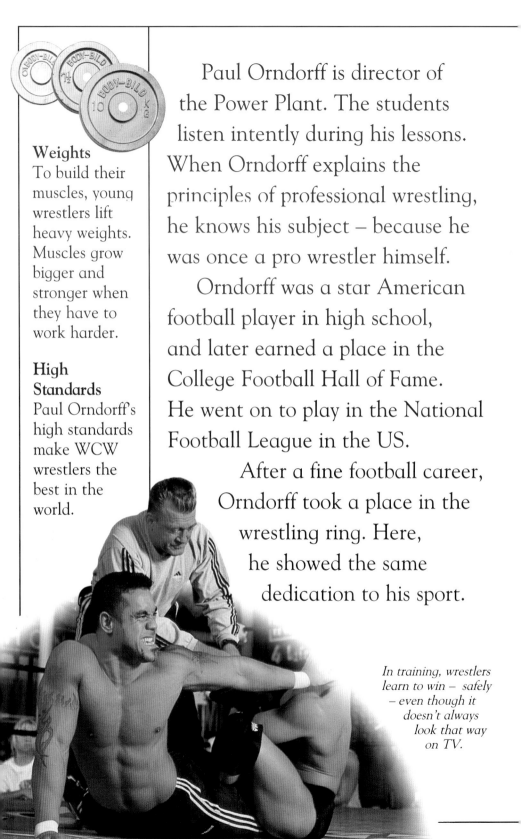

Weights
To build their muscles, young wrestlers lift heavy weights. Muscles grow bigger and stronger when they have to work harder.

High Standards
Paul Orndorff's high standards make WCW wrestlers the best in the world.

Paul Orndorff is director of the Power Plant. The students listen intently during his lessons. When Orndorff explains the principles of professional wrestling, he knows his subject – because he was once a pro wrestler himself.

Orndorff was a star American football player in high school, and later earned a place in the College Football Hall of Fame. He went on to play in the National Football League in the US.

After a fine football career, Orndorff took a place in the wrestling ring. Here, he showed the same dedication to his sport.

In training, wrestlers learn to win – safely – even though it doesn't always look that way on TV.

Orndorff quickly became one of wrestling's most popular "bad guys". His matches against Hulk Hogan drew record audiences all over the United States.

Orndorff captured the WCW TV title in 1993, wrestling under the nickname "Mr Wonderful".

He also picked up three tag team championship belts with two different partners during his time as one of WCW's finest wrestlers.

The Cat
Ernest "The Cat" Miller was a karate champion before he joined the Power Plant to study wrestling skills.

In the mid-1990s, Orndorff left the wrestling spotlight. He wanted to pass his knowledge to a new generation of athletes. He became director of the Power Plant, and devised a unique training course for WCW hopefuls.

In this gruelling training routine, students get lessons in discipline and physical conditioning. They even learn a little humility. Those who make it emerge with a great potential for success, and a respect for the business of pro wrestling.

"We're always recruiting," Orndorff says. "But it's hard, because the talent pool is limited. I used to run three-day open tryouts, testing young men for their heart and guts. Within 45 minutes, most candidates would quit."

These days, Orndorff prefers to review tapes of would-be students.

He is always looking for athletes like Goldberg, who have a history in professional sports, because they are more disciplined. Other stars who have caught Orndorff's eye are Kevin Nash and The Wall.

Kevin Nash
This former heavyweight champion played professional basketball in Europe before he became a wrestler.

The Wall
This star had all the qualities Paul Orndorff looked for in a young athlete. These are size, power, speed, discipline, and a physique straight out of a superhero comic book!

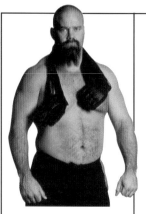

Tank Abbott
When he was asked about the toughest challenge of his life, Tank quickly replied: "Training at the Power Plant!"

David Flair
David is the son of wrestling legend Ric Flair. He emerged from his father's shadow thanks to his work at the Power Plant.

Orndorff analyses every wrestling manoeuvre in his lessons. He teaches young wrestlers how to keep safe in the ring, and how to win a match without injuring fellow wrestlers.

"After completing our Power Plant programme, my boys are two or three times more conditioned than most of our current athletes," Orndorff points out.

But wrestling moves and conditioning are not enough. The Power Plant also focuses on the mental strength needed to win in WCW. And that's where the head trainer, Sgt Buddy Lee Parker, comes in.

"Sarge" was a wrestler for 13 years himself, but now he uses his expertise in the training rooms at the Power Plant. This is where he helps Paul Orndorff spot future champions.

"If you have the right attitude and are willing to go the extra mile too, you have a shot," says Sarge.

He stresses that the mental discipline he teaches is just as important as the physical exercise.

"You have to be ready," he says. "You must have a good head on your shoulders to make it."

WCW beginnings

You've put in months of hard work at the Power Plant. You've pushed yourself to the limit and built up your muscles, your heart and your lungs.

Strength and balance
It's not enough to strengthen muscles. For each muscle that is built up, the opposite muscle must also be strengthened, for balance. So, if an athlete works on his biceps (top of the arm) he must also build up his triceps (bottom of the arm).

Now, you can endure even the toughest match, no matter how long, or how difficult your opponent.

You've listened carefully to Paul Orndorff and Sarge, and faced every demand with all your heart. You've shown that that you've got the stamina, discipline, and intelligence to be a champion.

Congratulations – it's time to graduate with honour from the Power Plant.

Now the *really* hard part begins!

Welcome to WCW.

Even the best graduates from the Power Plant must begin at the bottom of the WCW ladder. And there's a world of difference between training and stepping into the ring for your first match before a crowd of thousands, and millions of riveted TV viewers.

Setting up
The wrestling excitement you see on TV takes a lot of preparation, and not just by the wrestlers! A crew works for hours to set up the ring, the lighting, and the music systems.

Debut
Many of today's most famous wrestlers made their debut on *Monday Nitro.* The TV show can make or break wrestling careers in the space of two hours!

For some first-timers, starting a career in pro wrestling can be quite a shock. This was not the case, however, for former World Heavyweight Champion, Goldberg.

He spent four months training at the Power Plant. He built up his body, boosted his mental discipline, and learned the moves that would take him to the top.

Goldberg made his debut on *Monday Nitro,* September 22, 1997. His opponent was an experienced heavyweight wrestler named Hugh Morrus (now called General Rection). However, Morrus was totally unprepared for the rookie he faced in the ring.

It only took minutes for Goldberg to get the upper hand. The hard work, sweat, and sacrifice paid off as Goldberg pinned Morrus.

The match was over and victory number one was under Goldberg's belt. The first stepping stone was in place. He was on his way to becoming a WCW champion!

General Rection
Wild man General Rection likes to leap through the air, doing high-flying somersaults!

The crowd applaud Goldberg after another triumph. The superstar heavyweight went on to win over 170 matches in a row!

Sid Vicious
Sid Vicious had a big impact on WCW from the moment of his debut. Vicious started as half of the tag team called the Skyscrapers. This hulk combines power with personality to dominate in the ring. He has often been acclaimed as the "Future of Wrestling".

Some wrestlers have an international career before they sign up with WCW. Lance Storm (*right*) was a globe-trotting professional. He was born in Canada and won wrestling stardom in Austria, then Japan. His tag team, "The Thrillseekers", dominated tag team championships in the Far East.

Storm was then in a second tag team, "The Impact Players". When that team split up, he decided to go solo with WCW.

Storm won his early WCW matches using his brains and technical skill. His success came because he was a better wrestler than his opponents, not because he used tricks or weapons.

His experience and hard work led to him winning the WCW US title from Buff Bagwell in July 2000.

Lance Storm pins The Cat to the mat.

Heavyweights

The biggest achievement in professional wrestling is to win a championship belt. It's the payback for all the training and hours in the weights room. All the aches, pains, and defeats are worth it for this.

Although there are several different kinds of championship, many fans feel the ultimate achievement is to become the WCW Heavyweight Champion of the World.

Heavyweight champs, like Goldberg, Sting, and Jeff Jarrett, are perhaps the most admired wrestlers on Earth... although fans of the cruiserweight grappler Rey Mysterio, Jr. might disagree!

Sting
Sting captured his first world championship at the Great American Bash in 1990, taking the title from Ric Flair.

Goldberg's championship belt is engraved with his name.

To compete in the heavyweight division, a wrestler must weigh over 118 kilos. Many heavyweights weigh 130 or even 140 kilos.

Ric Flair won the first WCW world heavyweight belt, in 1991. Since then, only the very best have attained it. Winners of the heavyweight belt are recognized publicly as the best wrestlers in the world.

Jeff Jarrett won the WCW US and world heavyweight titles.

Kevin Nash won the WCW world heavyweight title three times!

King Rey
Rey is often called the "King of the Cruiserweights".

Kidman has won the WCW cruiserweight title twice!

Cruiserweights

To try for a cruiserweight title, wrestlers must weigh under 118 kilos. The best-known champs in this division are Kidman, Lt Loco, and Rey Mysterio, Jr.

Rey Mysterio, Jr. is a favourite with wrestling fans. He uses daredevil, high-flying aerial manoeuvres which bring a fast, athletic style of wrestling to WCW.

Rey has dazzled his fans and confused his opponents with speed and strategy. He proves you don't have to be big to be champ. Despite his size, Rey is not afraid to take on even the largest WCW heavyweights – and win! He has beaten Kevin Nash and Bam Bam Bigelow. That's why they call him "Giant Killer!"

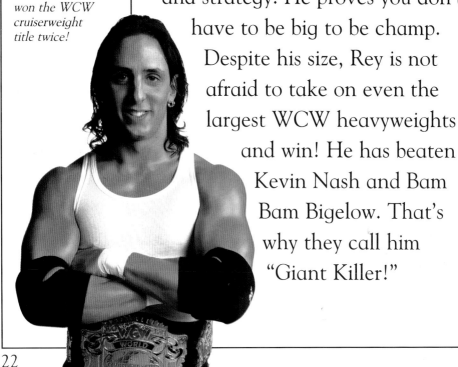

Corporal Cajun Although he hasn't won a title yet, Corporal Cajun may be the future of the cruiserweight division. In 1998, he was the only man out of 22 to survive the Power Plant's tryout. Cajun will surely wear a title belt soon.

Rey's acrobatic skills triumphed when he defeated Dean Malenko and won his first cruiserweight title in 1996. To date, he has won four more WCW cruiserweight titles. He's also won tag team belts, one with Kidman and one with Konnan.

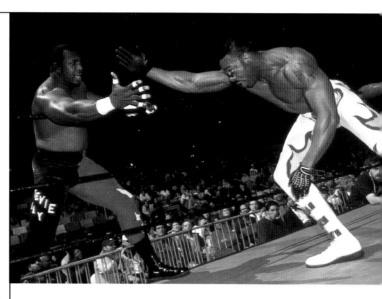

Harlem Heat
Brothers Booker T. and Stevie Ray wrestled as Harlem Heat. Together they won 10 tag team titles, the most in WCW history. They defeated wrestlers of all styles, including powerhouses, brawlers, and high-flyers.

Brothers in arms
Rick and Scott Steiner captured six WCW tag team titles during their time as a duo. As solo wrestlers, Scott – also known as "Big Poppa Pump" – won the WCW US title three times. Rick has taken three TV titles and one US title.

Tag teams

There have been many great WCW tag teams over the years. Harlem Heat and the Steiner Brothers both dominated the division. But the tag team known as Kronik – made up of Brian Adams and Bryan Clark – may be the future of WCW tag team wrestling. And for this terrible twosome, the future is now!

They are two of the most powerful men in WCW, and they have formed a partnership that may be unbeatable.

After a few months as a team, they won the WCW World Tag Team Championship in May 2000. They defeated The Franchise and The Wall before an enormous *Monday Nitro* TV audience.

A month later, they lost the title to Chuck Palumbo and Shawn Stasiak on *Thunder.* On July 9, at the Bash at the Beach pay-per-view event, they won the title back. Kronik are here to stay!

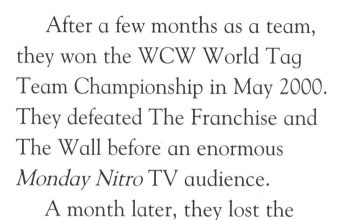

Kronik talent
Adams is a martial arts expert while Clark may be the strongest man in WCW and can easily lift other wrestlers above his head!

Kronik could rule the tag team division for years to come.

Booker T.
Booker T. had to become a solo wrestler when his brother, Stevie Ray, left their tag team. Booker T. saw this setback as a challenge. He persevered and went on to become the WCW World Heavyweight Champion.

Positive attitude

Everything you do in life – whether it's schoolwork, playing sports, or learning a new skill – requires a positive attitude in order to do it well. Just being able to do something can only get you so far. The approach you take in your own mind gets you the rest of the way. This is never more true than in the world of WCW wrestling.

When young wrestlers enter the Power Plant, Paul Orndorff and Sarge tell them that mental training matters as much as weight lifting. And a wrestler needs a lot of mental strength during his career in WCW.

Every time a wrestler loses a match or a championship title, he must somehow find the mental power needed to bounce back from defeat. Sometimes he has to return from an injury that threatens his career, or an unexpected defeat. Sometimes he returns after the wrestlers he thought were his friends have betrayed him. All these "comebacks" require a great deal of determination.

The Total Package took part in 3000 matches without being injured. When he was finally hurt, it took a different kind of strength for him to come back and fight again.

Hulk Hogan
Even Hulk Hogan needs a strong-minded approach. He has won, lost, and regained the championship title no fewer than eight times! Talk about a tough attitude!

Kidman
Kidman must rely on his willpower, and intelligence, to defeat much bigger rivals. He has already won the WCW cruiserweight title. Now he plans to win the heavyweight championship! That's belief in yourself!

Goldberg is a great example of a man with the right mental attitude. He enjoyed wrestling's longest winning streak – over 170 victories in a row! But, like all good things, his reign of triumph eventually came to an end.

In December 1998, at the annual *Starrcade* event, Goldberg clashed with Kevin Nash in a "no disqualification" match. It meant that neither wrestler could be disqualified for breaking the rules, whatever happened in the ring.

During the match, some of Nash's friends came into the ring to help him. They brought an illegal weapon, too. Goldberg went down. His winning streak was over.

But drawing on the same mental toughness that carried him through his victories, Goldberg came back. By January 1999 he was destroying the competition once again.

Once, an imposter dressed up as Sting and attacked Sting's tag team partners. The other wrestlers believed their attacker was the real Sting. They turned their backs on the superstar, leaving him hurt and alone.

When the truth was finally revealed, Sting's mental strength allowed him to put the event behind him. He returned to the ring in top form.

Ric Flair

Ric Flair has been wrestling for nearly 30 years. That's longer than anyone else in the WCW! He's suffered devastating losses, yet his positive attitude has allowed him to hold more titles than any other wrestler in history.

Back from the brink

The road to becoming a WCW champion is never straightforward or easygoing. As in any sport, injuries occur and throw unwelcome obstructions in the way to the top.

What does it take to come back from the brink of a career-ending injury? Ask Sting. In February 1990, Sting was one of the hottest rising stars in WCW. His gaze was firmly set on winning the heavyweight championship.

Then, in one painful moment, his world shattered. During a match in Texas, US, Sting tore his patella tendon. This tissue connects the leg muscle to the knee.

Sting's knee had to be rebuilt by surgeons. It was months before he could even think of wrestling again. Lesser men might have quit. But not this fierce competitor.

Buff's stuff
Buff Bagwell severely injured his neck during a match with Rick Steiner in 1998. Millions of viewers saw the accident on *Thunder*. It took 10 months and three surgeries before Buff finally returned to the ring in the best shape of his life, and his popularity at an all-time high.

After rest and healing, Sting began a gruelling series of exercises. He kept up his overall top condition, and gradually built up the muscles around his knee, too.

Kanyon
Injuries are no laughing matter. But some wrestlers fake injury to fool their opponents. Kanyon was thrown from the top of a steel cage and through a ramp by Mike Awesome. Kanyon pretended his injuries were serious in order to trick his former friend, Diamond Dallas Page.

A wrestler who wants to come back from an injury has to work hard at the gym.

Scott Steiner
Scott Steiner (*below*) won six WCW tag team titles alongside his brother Rick. Then he was hit with painful shoulder and back injuries. His amazing comeback led to a career in the renegade group, the nWo.

Injuries
Wrestlers who are mentally tough can survive injury to do battle another day.

Sting returned to action in July 1990, at the *Great American Bash* event. In his first match back, he tried for the heavyweight title!

The odds were stacked against Sting, but he was determined to win that belt. His battle with Ric Flair is still considered a classic. He broke free from Flair's Figure Four leg lock. Then, he used his Scorpion Deathlock to capture his first WCW World Championship.

He had not only come back, but he had captured the title in his return match.

Both mentally and physically, Sting was truly fit for the title.

The wrestler called The Franchise also made an awesome comeback.

The Franchise won the WCW tag team title with his partner, Ricky Steamboat. But then a terrible injury forced him to quit wrestling altogether.

It took him *two years* to recover. He came back as a solo grappler, and is now more popular than ever.

The Franchise
This guy is an outsider who has left the world of professional wrestling many times. In WCW, he was recently a major player in the renegade New Blood group. Believe it or not, during his two-year break, The Franchise was on the verge of going to medical school!

In the end, he decided to come back to wrestling.

Norman Smiley takes a knock from The Franchise.

Cruiserweight
Rey Mysterio,
Jr. used his
high-flying
acrobatics to
take down
the tattooed
heavyweight
Bam Bam
Bigelow in
a thrilling
match. It just
goes to show
that the bigger
they are, the
harder they
fall!

Fast and high-flying

They fly through the air with the greatest of ease. No, not trapeze artists. We're talking about the WCW cruiserweights!

As with the heavyweights, a tremendous amount of training goes into becoming a cruiserweight champion. They are smaller, lighter, and more acrobatic than the bulky heavyweights. Cruiserweights use tactics, agility, and speed to win matches, rather than bulk and brute strength.

This type of fast-paced aerial combat grew out of the exciting Mexican style of wrestling, known as "lucha libre". Its main force in WCW is the lightning-fast wrestler, Rey Mysterio, Jr.

Rey wasn't satisfied with simply beating everyone else in the cruiserweight division. So he took on some of the biggest, scariest heavyweights in WCW – and beat them! These included Kevin Nash and Bam Bam Bigelow.

Mysterio proves that with fitness and the right attitude, you can overcome any obstacle, however large, heavy, and obstinate!

Loyalty
Despite offers to join the outlaw nWo, Rey has remained loyal to WCW, even though at times he has had to battle four men all by himself!

Rey clubs Booker T. with Konnan!

Not all lucha libre stars are cruiserweights. Konnan is too big to qualify as a cruiserweight. Instead, this Mexican powerhouse has shown fans that lucha libre style can also work in the heavyweight division.

No one in WCW has more attitude than Konnan. He gave up a great deal to wrestle in the United States. In Mexico, he was a household name, not only as a wrestling star, but as a TV and movie star as well.

But Konnan believed in himself, and his abilities, and he was right. In the United States, he has captured the WCW world tag team title, the WCW United States title, and the WCW world television title.

Konnan has opened the door for other lucha libre stars to try for success in WCW.

Lt Loco
Another major force from Mexico is the cruiserweight Lt Loco. Born Chavo Guerrero, this high-flyer grew up in Mexico's most famous wrestling family. He quickly rose through the ranks of WCW to capture the cruiserweight title.

Crowbar
Oddly enough, David Flair, who used to carry a crowbar into the ring, fought with a tag team partner who called himself "Crowbar". Together, they won the WCW Tag Team Championship.

David Flair

Many of the topics mentioned in this book come together in the person of David Flair.

Family tradition? He's the son of legendary WCW great Ric Flair.

Cruiserweight? Well, his lightweight frame hardly puts him in the heavyweight division!

Training? Because he came into WCW as "Ric Flair's son", he began wrestling before he had fully trained in the physical and mental disciplines required for the sport. Now, several years into his career, David Flair spends time at the Power Plant, learning the skills he needs to mature into a serious wrestler.

Flair is one of the few wrestlers who held a title before he was ready for it. In 1999, David's father Ric was WCW president. Ric Flair stripped Scott Steiner of the WCW US title and handed it to his son! Flair's enemies (and there are plenty) became David Flair's enemies.

Because he was forced to fight before his training was complete, David began carrying a crowbar into the ring to make up for his inexperience.

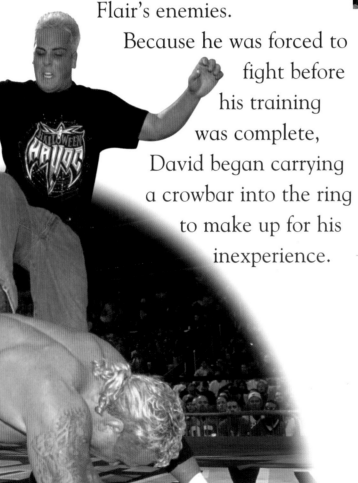

Role model
You might think that David Flair would want to copy his father's style in the ring. But the wrestler David would most like to copy is six-time tag team champion Arn Anderson (*above*). Anderson is one of the most respected professionals in wrestling.

Costumes

The WCW wrestler who is fit for the title is a complete package, and that package even extends to the costume he wears.

Costumes are about more than just showmanship and dazzle. They are statements about each wrestler's unique image and their wrestling personality.

Sting
Vampiro's biggest WCW rival, Sting, also wears white face paint. Sting didn't always look this way. Early in his career he had short blond hair!

One wrestler with an outrageous costume is Vampiro. His look is as unique a part of his image as his physique, and his finishing move.

Vampiro looks more like a creature from a horror movie than an athlete. Fiery dragon tattoos cover his chest, and white face paint makes him look like a ghost. His swirling black cape envelops his body like the shadows of night.

Vampiro creates a mood of mystery and menace. How could any opponent not be affected by his scary persona? Take one look at those eyes, that costume, and his overall image, and it's a wonder that any wrestler stays in the ring long enough to do battle with Vampiro!

Masked men
Rey Mysterio, Jr. was given his mask by his uncle, who was a wrestling superstar in Mexico.

Not all costumed wrestlers lean to the dark side. Ric Flair is well known for his tremendous wrestling skill and long career. And the former champ is also famous for his costumes!

Jung Dragons
The three-man tag team known as Jung Dragons wear black Ninja robes and masks. These add to the air of danger surrounding their high-flying, martial arts moves. The Jung Dragons even break into song and dance routines. It confuses their opponents and delights the crowd!

His elaborate, beaded robes glitter with golden light. His grand entrance adds to Flair's air of confidence. It is enough to undermine any opponent.

Speaking of gold, Disco looks as if he just stepped out of the 1970s! This heavyweight wrestler likes to wear silk shirts, bellbottom trousers, and matching vests in the ring. Gold chains hang around his neck. He's wrestled opponents while wearing tight leopard print trousers and orange ruffled shirts! And his hair is always perfectly groomed, reminding fans of John Travolta in the 1970s movie *Saturday Night Fever.*

Just don't let the costume fool you. Disco has worn gold around his waist, not just his neck, in the form of WCW cruiserweight and TV belts.

Disco Time
Disco has the clothes, the moves – and the music, too! He enters the arena with his theme song blaring, and dances to the disco beat!

Secrets of the stars

So now you know what goes into building a WCW champion. You learned everything there is to know about the champions you love to cheer on.

Right? Well, maybe not.

Did you know…

That when Rey Mysterio, Jr. first started to wrestle, he was only 16 years old? He used to do his homework in the locker room while waiting for matches to begin, and had already been wrestling for two years when he left school!

And did you know that Juventud Guerrara's father and Rey Mysterio's uncle were wrestling rivals in Mexico?

Did you know that Kevin Nash once featured in his own comic book? It was called "Nash" and it was about a futuristic hero.

Sting
When he's not wrestling, Sting loves to play volleyball. He's also fond of performing in front of the movie cameras. He's appeared in the films *Shutterspeed*, *The Real Reason (Men Commit Crimes)*, and *Ready To Rumble*.

Also, did you know that DDP videotapes all his matches so that he can study his every move later?

And finally, did you know that Goldberg and DDP are great friends, despite their epic battles in the ring?

Quick on the draw
When he's not in the arena, Corporal Cajun loves to draw. He regularly provides cartoons for WCW magazine.

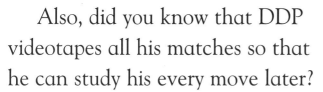

Hulk Hogan
Hulk Hogan, the most well-known wrestler in the world, lives by these words. "Never let anyone say you can't do something. Follow your dreams, no matter how tough it may be to achieve them, and you'll be successful."

Hulk Hogan knocks Sting to the mat. The two have met in many memorable matches. They just may be the most famous wrestlers in the world!

Last words

All wrestlers have some things in common. They must devote a lot of time to hard work, conditioning, mental toughness, and learning their way around the ring. Or else their WCW careers will be over before you can say *"Monday Nitro"*.

But wrestlers all differ, too. Being an individual is a key part of their success, both in the ring and with the fans. So each top wrestler has a different answer to the question, "What makes a wrestler fit for the title?"

Goldberg says it's concentration. Mike Awesome says it's conditioning, but Kevin Nash believes that size is the key to success.

Rey Mysterio, Jr. puts his success down to agility, while Sting relies on the element of surprise. And Scott Steiner claims it's down to muscles, muscles, and more muscles!

So what does all this add up to? Perhaps, that the key to success is believing in yourself. Believe in your abilities and your individual worth... then you'll be fit for anything!

Big heart
Kidman says: "The size of your body is not what matters. What's important is the size of your heart."

Buff Bagwell and Jeff Jarrett share a victory.

Glossary

Aerial
In the air.

Aerobic
Any activity that
increases the rate
at which a person's
heart beats.

Aspiring
Hoping to reach
an aim or goal.

Attain
To achieve; to reach
a goal.

Contender
Someone who has a good
chance of achieving a
goal.

Debut
The first time someone
appears somewhere.
In this case, the first
time someone appears
as a WCW wrestler.

Disqualified
Removed from a contest
because of cheating.

Endure
To bear or put up
with something difficult
or unpleasant.

Epic
A long and grand
story or journey.

Graduate
A student who has
finished a course of
studies; or, to leave
school after finishing
your studies.

Grappler
Wrestler.

Grappling
Wrestling.

Gridiron
American football field.

Gruelling
Very difficult.

Humility
To be humble,
to not go around
praising yourself.

Imposter
A person who pretends
to be someone else by
using a deception.

Mature
To develop into
something stronger
or better.

Obstinate
Stubborn.

Obstructions
Things that block a
path or get in the way.

Overcome
To move past barriers in
order to achieve a goal.

Perseverance
Continuing to work
toward a goal, despite
barriers or difficulties.

Persona
An identity that a
person creates for him
or herself.

Pretender
Someone who wants
a high position and
believes he or she can
achieve that position.

Professional, or "pro"
In sport, someone
who earns his or her
living through sport.

Psychology
The study of the mind,
which tries to explain
why people behave the
way they do.

Reign
A period of time during
which someone is ruler.

Renegade
A person, or group,
who breaks the rules.

Rookie
A first-timer; or,
an athlete who is
competing in his or her
first year in a sport.

Sacrifice
To give up.

Stamina
Staying power; the
ability to keep going.

Strategy
A plan someone comes
up with to help them
succeed with a difficult
activity or project.

Undermine
To work to disrupt or
destroy something
secretly.